Gabe's Hero

Written By: Lady Charmae Ferebee
Illustrated By: Adam

This book is dedicated to the men in my life. My husband and best friend Xavier andmy beautiful sons, Gabriel and my sweet angel-baby Isaiah.

I love you all and Isaiah you will forever live on through us.

Rest peacefully sweet baby.

Gabe walked over to his mommy and daddy sitting on the couch, "Mommy why are you so sad? Why are you crying?"

Mommy smiled sadly at Gabe and said "My handsome Gabe I'm sad because your brother is gone."

Gabe asked "Where has he gone?"

Mommy took a second looking at daddy then said, "He's sleeping."

Gabe then asked, "Well can't we wake him up?"

Mommy shook her head, "No my love, he is sleep in heaven."

Gabe smiled, "Well let's go visit him then!"

Daddy reached out and pulled Gabe onto his lap, "No little buddy, we can't visit him. Heaven doesnt allow visitors."

Gabe then lowered his head, "So why did he leave?"

Gabe asked in a small voice,
"Did he not want to be with us?"

Mommy reached over and hugged Gabe tightly,
"Oh no Gabe, he wanted to be here with us so
much! But he had to leave because he helped
mommy heal."

With big brown eyes, filling with tears Gabe
asked, "What's wrong with your body?"

Mommy inhaled slowly, then Daddy said" You
know how we pray to God for help sometimes?"

Gabe nods.

"Well, mommy's body was hiding a big scar that could hurt her badly, and baby brother asked God to help her. God gave baby brother the power to help mommy but that would mean baby brother would have to stay with God."

With eyes filled with awe, Gabe asked "My brother had powers?"

Mommy nodded then said,
"Yes, God gave him the power to help mommy and heal her body."

In an astonished voice,
Gabe whispered "Wow!"

"Yes Gabe, baby brother loved us
so much that he decided to stay
with God in heaven and save
mommy's life. And from there he
can watch over us and keep us safe."
Daddy explained.

Looking between both his parents Gabe exclaimed, "Don't be sad mommy, baby brother was a superhero!" He jumped down and ran to his room, coming back with his Black Panther action figure in hand.

"Just like the Black Panther my brother can save the world, just like he saved mommy." Gabe remarked, holding the action figure up for his parents to see.

Kneeling down to the floor, Daddy raised his hand and Gabe gave him a high five, "Yea buddy just like Black Panther, baby brother saved mommy. A true hero, your hero."

Jumping into his father's arms Gabe hugged him tightly and whispered, "Yea my own real life hero, my brother." Mommy then kneeled down and joined in on the hug, kissing Gabe on top of the head.

ISAIAH

"My own hero, my brother." Gabe whispered as he played with his toys.